PRAISE FOR MALLIKA CHOPRA AND *JUST BREATHE*:

"A solid addition to collections in need of meditation and mindfulness titles for tweens."

—*School Library Journal*

"Adults sharing mindfulness with children and preteens will find a treasure trove of scripts for guided practice."

—*Kirkus Reviews*

"I wish I had learned to *Just Breathe* when I was younger. The lessons inside are priceless, and you will be able to use them for the rest of your life. All kids—and all adults—should read it."

—**Cara Natterson, pediatrician and *New York Times* bestselling author of The Care and Keeping of You series**

"*Just Breathe* is a gift for the whole family. With fun illustrations and simple steps, this book will empower you to feel more in control, to genuinely connect with others, and to approach life with peace and joy."

—**Dr. Shefali Tsabary, clinical psychologist and author of the *New York Times* bestseller *The Conscious Parent***

"*Just Breathe* is the book I wish I had growing up."

—**Tara Stiles, founder of Strala Yoga**

"Chopra opens the door to a direct discovery of how good it feels to be less anxious, healthier, and experience a more balanced way of life. Starting meditation young, in adolescence, is a lifelong set up for health, peace, and thriving."

—**Dr. Lisa Miller, author of *The Spiritual Child: The New Science of Parenting for Health and Lifelong Thriving*, and professor and founder, Spirituality and Mind-Body Institute, Columbia University, Teachers College**

"A charming and engaging book of life skills that speaks directly to tweens themselves, not through intermediaries like their parents or teachers. Mallika's wonderful new book is an essential addition to your child's bookshelf!"

—**Susan Kaiser Greenland, author of *Mindful Games* and *The Mindful Child***

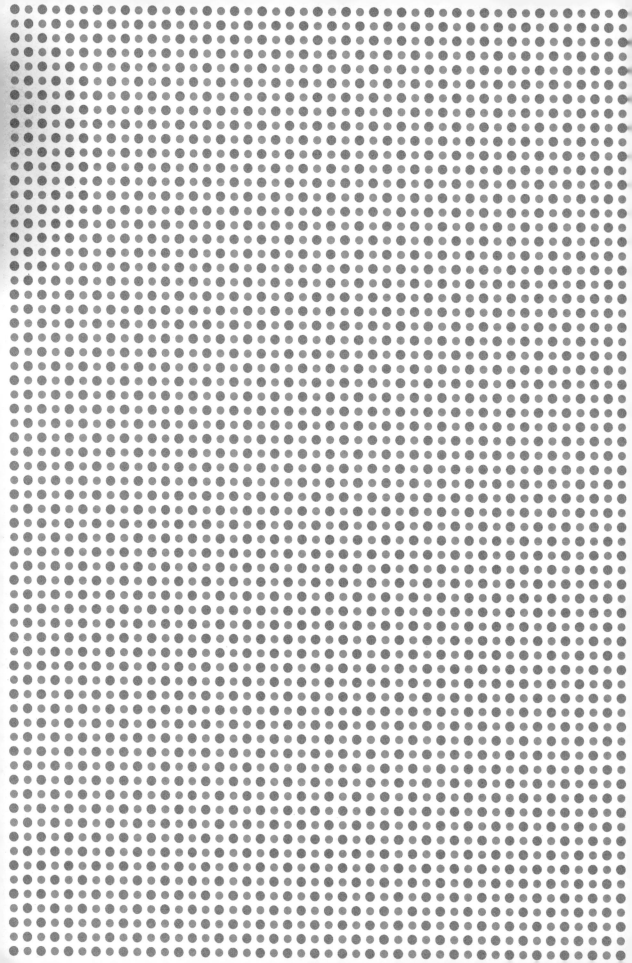

JUST FEEL

HOW TO BE STRONGER, HAPPIER, HEALTHIER, AND MORE

MALLIKA CHOPRA

author of *Just Breathe*

Illustrated by Brenna Vaughan

Afterword by Deepak Chopra

RP|KIDS
PHILADELPHIA

Running Press Kids
Hachette Book Group
1290 Avenue of the Americas, New York, NY 10104
www.runningpress.com/rpkids
@RP_Kids

Printed in China

First Edition: October 2019

Published by Running Press Kids, an imprint of Perseus Books, LLC,
a subsidiary of Hachette Book Group, Inc. The Running Press Kids name and logo
is a trademark of the Hachette Book Group.

The Hachette Speakers Bureau provides a wide range of authors for speaking events.
To find out more, go to www.hachettespeakersbureau.com or call (866) 376-6591.

The publisher is not responsible for websites (or their content)
that are not owned by the publisher.

Print book cover and interior design by Frances J. Soo Ping Chow.

Library of Congress Control Number: 2019932185

ISBNs: 978-0-7624-9474-3 (paperback), 978-0-7624-9473-6 (ebook)

1010

10 9 8 7 6 5 4 3 2 1

TO MY FAMILY.

I realize how lucky I am to be
on this journey with you.
I am, and will be, forever grateful.

TABLE OF CONTENTS

• • • • •

TAKE ACTION . . . 75

WHY I WROTE THIS BOOK

If you are reading this book, it means you are old enough to be aware of your feelings and how things affect you. It means you are ready to be responsible, to express what you want, and to make decisions about how you live.

Perhaps someone bought this book for you and you are looking at it with an adult. Or maybe you are opening it by yourself where you live, in your classroom, or at the library. Perhaps a family member, friend, teacher, or counselor thought it would be a good book for you to read.

Maybe you were *excited* to open the pages because of the illustrations. Or you were feeling *sad* and thought the title was interesting. Perhaps you were *annoyed* that someone was trying to make you read this book! You may have had other feelings, as well.

Whatever the reason, this book is now in your hands, and now it's your choice to read it, think about what it has to say, and test its ideas in your own life.

Knowing that you have choices is actually one of the reasons I wrote this book.

When I was young, my parents taught me that I was responsible for my actions and reactions, particularly when it came to my feelings. My parents didn't expect me to be *happy* or *excited* all the time. Rather, they let me feel *pride* and *joy* in my accomplishments, and they let me reflect on my failures, too. They let me feel *sad*, *angry*, and *frustrated* so that I could learn how to use my feelings to be a stronger person. They taught me to be aware of the many emotions we all experience in life and to make choices about how I reacted to them.

My parents taught me that feelings are treasures—my feelings helped me discover what made me unique, which helped me figure out what I wanted in my life. I am grateful to my parents for giving me tools to be comfortable with and to accept my feelings.

As I grew older, I realized what a gift my parents had given me; I felt I could appreciate the good times but also get through tough times. As a mother, I have tried to teach my daughters—Tara and Leela—that they, too, will have lots of experiences; they will feel *strong* at times and *uncertain* at other times.

In this book, I am sharing some of the ideas and tools that we use to support each other's feelings and to manage our days. I have now also learned so much from other experts and am honored to share these ideas with you. I hope you find them helpful.

Mallika

INTRODUCTION

Take a deep breath, right now.

Breathe in. Pause. And breathe out.

Ask yourself: *How do I feel?* Right now, in this moment: *How do I feel?*

You don't need to share the answer with anyone—this is a question just for you.

For some, when you ask this question, you may think, *I feel great!*

For others, you may feel really *sad* or *angry* or *lonely*.

Or you may even be *confused* and not sure how you feel. Maybe that makes you feel *scared*. Or maybe that makes you feel *at peace*.

Perhaps, you think, *I feel nothing*.

Most people may feel one way right now and completely different an hour from now or tomorrow. Or perhaps they feel more than one feeling at the same time.

That is normal.

Every person in the world goes through ups and downs. Every person feels *happy* and *sad*. And for some people, when they are sad, it is hard to remember that they were ever happy.

Your feelings don't define you. They come and go, just like the clouds drift in and out of the sky. Sometimes the clouds are light wisps and seem to blow freely and effortlessly in the wind; and other times, the clouds are dark and look heavy and rainy. The clouds, like your feelings, keep changing across the sky, and they may look different at times, but the sky is still just the sky. Similarly, you are more than your feelings, and while they may seem overwhelming at times, with practice you can remember that you are the one who is experiencing feelings (like the sky) and that you can reflect and learn from them.

You can develop skills to become aware of your feelings and be more comfortable with them. You can also learn how to see the ways other people's emotions affect their lives—and maybe even yours! When you know what you are feeling, understand why you are feeling that way, and have ways to manage the tough times and celebrate the good ones, you will have more energy and power to get through every day.

> **You are not your feelings. You are the one who is experiencing your feelings and deciding what to do about them!**

HOW TO USE THIS BOOK

- - - - - - - - - - - - -

Deep down inside, most of us want to be healthy, happy, connected to others, and valuable to our friends, family, and community.

This book assumes that no one is perfect—you have strengths and weaknesses; you make mistakes; you like to do some things and don't like to do other things; and you, like everyone else, sometimes need help from others. This book helps you to know that you are strong and intelligent, even if you don't feel it all the time.

This book is also about letting you know that you are resilient—you already have the power inside you to get back up when things don't go your way or when you are struggling. Hopefully, the information in this book will help you feel stronger, find inspiration, make good choices, and connect with others in real, meaningful ways.

Here is the basic idea you'll find in this book: *If you **know** how you feel, you can make smart **choices** and **act** to create the life you want.*

This book presents facts, ideas, and exercises for you to:

• Know—
be aware of your body, mind, surroundings,
desires, and feelings.

• Choose—
what you focus on, how you look at the world,
how you communicate, and how you want to live your life.

• Act—
to smartly manage your time, interact with others,
set goals, and do things that make you happy and successful.

Don't feel like you need to read this book in strict order from beginning to end. Rather, you can flip through the pages and see what may be relevant to your life today and read those sections first.

And while this book is written for you, you can also use it to educate your parents, teachers, and other adults in your life about your feelings and choices.

Ready? Let's begin!

What Makes You Feel Good

• • • • •

Well-being is about feeling good about your body and mind, your relationships, your community, and your world (the planet).

Some anchors in your life make you feel safe, happy, and connected to others. These include:

- being in an environment and around people you trust
- feeling good emotionally and physically
- having enough energy to get through the day
- feeling okay with experiencing a range of emotions—happy, sad, angry, frustrated, inspired, scared, excited
- feeling like you can honestly express yourself to others
- knowing how to deal with mood swings, anxiety, and stress
- having good relationships

But, you can also add:

• feeling like you matter and can contribute
something helpful to the people in your life or to the planet

• being part of a community

• having a spiritual connection

In this book, you will break down the different parts of your well-being and also explore tools to help you feel more in control of shaping your life.

You will be asked to think about what it takes to keep going when life gets tough, and hopefully you will find ways to help you think of how you can create the life you want—both now and in the future as you grow older.

What You Control

• ○ • ○ •

While there are some things in your life you can control, it is important to recognize that there are lots of things that you *cannot* control.

For example, you probably can't control the makeup of your family, where you or your family lives, or how much money your family makes. Maybe you feel like you have no control over the quality of the food you eat or the air around you, what school you go to, or your parents' schedules.

There are things that maybe you *can* control that will make you feel better—how much you sleep, eat, study, play, or connect with others. If you can figure out what you can control in your life, then you can take responsibility and be motivated to change those things so you can be stronger, healthier, and happier.

Know

EXERCISE:

WHAT CAN I CONTROL?

- - - - - - - - - - - -

Time Needed: **5 MINUTES**
Location: **A QUIET PLACE WHERE YOU CAN THINK**
Materials Needed: **A PIECE OF PAPER AND A PEN OR PENCIL**

Look at this list of things that may be part of your life:

- *My family*
- *My room*
- *My house*
- *My friends*
- *My school*
- *My neighborhood*
- *My body*
- *My health*
- *What I eat and drink*
- *How I move*
- *How much I exercise*

- *How much I sleep*
- *How much time I spend on homework*
- *How much I do extracurricular things (sports, music, dance, or other)*
- *How I spend my free time*
- *My mood*
- *My feelings*
- *My goals*
- *My words*
- *How I treat others*

Think about the things that you can control or influence on this list.

Write those down on your piece of paper.

Each one of us can control different things in our life, and sometimes these things can be due to different circumstances. Be honest with yourself about what you know you control for yourself, what you may be able to influence or suggest to others, and what you know you can't control.

For now, just having this list will help you become more aware of the parts of your life that you can change or adjust when needed. As you go through this book, you can try to also focus on things you may be able to influence.

The fact is that sometimes you can control or change some things in your life and other times you can't. For example, you may get sick and your doctor recommends you rest—you can't control being sick in that moment, but you can decide to follow the doctor's recommendations so you can feel better soon.

Your moods may also swing from feeling happy to frustrated to depressed to lonely all in one day. But if you know that moods come and go, and that sometimes you can influence them, maybe that will make your day just a bit easier.

For those things you can't control (either all the time or just sometimes), planning in advance about how you can feel safer may make life easier for you.

You can also think about who you could brainstorm with to make a situation better. Perhaps this can be your parents, a sibling, a teacher, or a school counselor. They may not be able to change much, either, but at least you'll feel like someone knows more about your situation. You may not feel as alone as you once thought you were.

You are Safe

• • • • •

Safety is one of your most basic needs.

There are two kinds of ways you can feel safe: *physically* and *emotionally*.

Feeling *physically* safe means that you feel comfortable around the people you live with and with whom you interact throughout the day. It means that when you go to school or walk in your neighborhood, you feel secure and don't have any fear. It also means you feel safe around other people and in your body.

Hopefully, you don't have to think too much about your safety on a daily basis. But as you get older, it will be wise for you to know how to create as safe an environment for yourself as possible.

For many kids, physical safety isn't a reality. It's not fair, because every child deserves to live in a safe place. To feel as physically as safe as you can, you can turn to trusted adults for help. Ask a parent, teacher, or mentor how to get through your days as safely as possible.

You can be smart about your choices—how you walk to school, what type of people you choose to hang around with, and where you hang out when you are free. And, if other people are making you feel unsafe, like bullies at school or even an adult who you know should not be hurting you, turn to a counselor or someone you can trust for help.

There are things you can do to feel more physically safe in your body, too. You can help guide your parents on what foods are best to eat; you can drink more water; and you can sleep more. You can exercise each day and find ways to feel stronger in your body. You can try breathing practices to calm down and learn how to meditate or be aware of your body to help with anxiety. And if you are not feeling safe in your body or with how others are treating you, sometimes you may need to change your interactions with others and say no. This can be very scary, but you have the right to say no to anyone.

Feeling *emotionally* safe means you are comfortable being with others and sharing your feelings with them. Sometimes it's really hard to feel emotionally safe—you may feel terrified to express your opinions or hurts or hopes with someone else. You may feel disappointed by friends or family. You may also feel that you are scared to be around certain people. This is normal, too.

If you can find even one person you can trust, this can make your life so much better. Sometimes it takes time to feel safe around others. Sometimes the scariest feeling in the world is to tell someone that you don't feel safe or that someone you love or know may not be safe. But doing so could change your life—you can be brave and change your life or the life of someone else.

Loving adults, friends, siblings, teachers, and counselors are good people to turn to when you need some help.

Know

DO I FEEL SAFE?

Time Needed: **2 MINUTES**
Location: **ANYWHERE**

Take a deep breath right now.

Ask yourself: Do I feel physically safe most of the time?

Then ask yourself: Do I feel emotionally safe most of the time?

If the answer to both questions is YES, take a deep breath and say to yourself, "I am grateful that I feel safe today."

If the answer is NO or MAYBE to one or both of these questions, first just take a deep breath in and out. Now, think about why you are not feeling safe—perhaps a relationship doesn't feel right; or maybe you feel out of control; or maybe someone spoke to you in a way that made you feel uncomfortable. Breathe deeply again, and say to yourself, "I am going to do what I can to feel safer in my life."

Think about someone you can brainstorm with—a sibling, friend, parent, teacher, mentor, school or community counselor—to find ways you can feel safer in your life.

Asking for help makes you powerful.

Just Feel

Your Body

· · · · ·

An important part of a healthy and happy life is to feel as physically good as you can.

You were born with a body that is unique to you. While there are some things about your body that you can't change, you do have a lot of control over how you take care of your body.

Taking care of your body is one of the most important steps to feeling good, to having a clear mind, and to gathering energy to do what you want to do in your life.

You may have a physical disability or illness that requires you to live life a little differently than others. And, because of this, you may actually be more aware of your body than others. Or, you may be a dancer or athlete who regularly pushes your body. You may be aware of how movement makes you feel better but also know when you have pushed yourself too far.

You may or may not be aware of how food and water affect your mood and physical well-being. You can make the choice to learn more about what nurtures your body, helps you grow, and gives you a clear mind. You can also learn to pay attention to what your body is telling you. Your body gives you messages about your reactions to food and movement but also about your reactions to your feelings. You can learn to pay attention to your gut feelings: goosebumps, tummy aches, chills, headaches, and other physical messages your body may be sending to you.

No matter your physical state, if you know how your body is feeling, you can make choices to feel as good as possible.

Here is a body awareness exercise to help you become aware of how you feel physically.

Know

EXERCISE:

BODY AWARENESS EXERCISE

- - - - - - - - - - - -

Time Needed: **10 MINUTES**
Location: **SOMEWHERE YOU CAN LIE DOWN,
PERHAPS IN YOUR BED**

Lie down comfortably on your back. Use a pillow under your head or knees if it makes you more comfortable.

Close your eyes.

Note that when you are comfortable like this, you may fall asleep. If you do fall asleep, pay attention to the message your body is sending you. You may be really tired and probably need to get more rest at night.

Take a deep breath and put your attention on your whole body. Feel your body breathing air in and out.

(Throughout this exercise, if you need to adjust your body, go ahead and move. You don't need to be perfectly still!)

Notice if there is a part of your body where you feel tension or even aches and pains.

Put your attention on that part of your body, and say to yourself: I FEEL YOU.

You can even be more specific and say: I FEEL YOU, ANKLE! I FEEL YOU, LOWER BACK!

As you focus on areas that may need some attention, take a few deep breaths. If it is helpful to stretch or massage that part of your body, go ahead.

Imagine the air you are breathing in going to that part of your body and massaging it.

You may even envision the air as a certain color—like a light blue—and see how it goes through the part of your body that is seeking attention.

Once you feel you have covered the areas that need attention, take another deep breath.

Open your eyes.

For the day, you may come back now and again and send a breath to the parts of your body that are asking for attention. You may find that envisioning the breath as a color going through you helps you be more aware.

And, once you are aware of how your body is feeling, you can try different adjustments to how you sit, stand, move, exercise, and eat to keep that part of your body feeling good and healthy.

You can then do the body awareness exercise again and see if you feel differently.

Maybe you will find another part of your body that now needs attention!

What Your Body Needs

· · · · ·

There are some important things your body needs to feel good.
These include:

- food
- water
- movement
- sleep

As you become more aware of your body, you can determine the best habits to feel as physically good as you can.

Here are suggestions from experts on how you can feel good:

Food

Eat nutritious food every day, such as fruits, vegetables, and protein. (Protein includes eggs, meat, cheese, yogurt, and beans.) Avoid food and drinks with too much sugar. When you get in the habit of having too much sugar as a kid, it's harder to stay healthy as you grow older. Sugar can affect your appetite and you can put on unhealthy weight if you consume too much. It also affects your moods—for some people, sugar makes you feel a burst of high energy, like you are really happy, followed by really low energy, like you are tired and moody.

Know

Water

Water nurtures your brain and your body. Often, headaches or body stress can be due to dehydration—that's when your body doesn't have enough water in it.

Think of your brain as a juicy fruit: it looks good and healthy when it has a lot of water and isn't dried up. Some experts recommend that you drink at least eight glasses of water a day to keep your body healthy and hydrated.

Movement

Moving makes your body feel good. Exercise, especially walking and stretching, can make your body strong and flexible, and this will ultimately make you happier. Sports, yoga, dance, and martial arts are great ways to move your body. Regardless of the body you have, you can always look for practical ways to add a little extra movement into your day, like cleaning your room, helping put the groceries away, or taking your dog on a walk.

Sleep

Never sacrifice sleep. Really, just don't do it. Figure out how to manage your time so that you get at least eight to nine hours of sleep every night. (As a kid, you actually may need even more than that.) Aside from the fact that you grow while you sleep, rest helps you avoid being in a bad mood, becoming depressed, and feeling nervous.

If you don't get enough sleep, talk to your parents, teachers, or caregivers about cutting back on extracurricular activities or homework so you have time to get more rest. Sleep is how you rejuvenate and heal your body, so you need to make sure you are getting enough of it, especially if you are very active all day.

Just Feel

EXERCISE:

BODY CARE CHECKLIST

- - - - - - - - - - -

Time Needed: **A FEW MOMENTS
THROUGHOUT THE DAY (3 DAYS TOTAL)**
Location: **SOMEWHERE QUIET AT THE END OF YOUR DAY**
Materials Needed: **3 PIECES OF PAPER AND A PEN**

In this exercise, you will keep a body journal for three days. Use one piece of paper for each day. You may want to consider doing this exercise with a friend, parent, or trusted adult who is also interested in becoming more aware of their habits.

On each piece of paper, write the following as a list: Sleep, Food, Water, and Movement. Keep space between each section.

Take this paper with you to school or wherever you go throughout the day so you can keep updating it.

Remember what time you went to bed and what time you woke up. Write the hours of sleep you got.

List all the foods you ate for the day. It is best to list these under each meal: breakfast, lunch, dinner, and snack.

Count how many glasses of water you drank during the day.

Write how you moved during the day and how much time you spent moving.

At the end of the day, before you go to sleep, look at how you approached the day.

Circle the healthy foods you ate.

Know

Write how many glasses of water you drank. (Don't count juice, milk, or soda.)

Circle how many hours of sleep you got. Did you reach eight hours?

How much did you move? Did you walk? Did you have PE class? Did you participate in any sports, martial arts, dance?

On the back of the paper, write or draw your reflections and think about how you could feel better tomorrow.

At the end of three days, review your list and see what you learned about how you take care of your body.

If you did this exercise with someone else, share what each of you learned. If you did it by yourself, find someone with whom you can share your thoughts.

Set a goal to adjust one thing to take better care of your body.

In one week, do the exercise again and see how you have changed your habit and how you may feel differently.

Your Mind

· · · · ·

Your mind is the part of you that experiences your emotions. It is where you experience the sensations, images, beliefs, memories, imaginations, and thoughts that make you happy, excited, sad, inspired, and fearful.

The funny thing about your mind is that you can't really find it. The mind is different from your brain.

Your brain and chemicals in your body react to and shape your mind. Here is a super simple explanation of how your mind works: When you are happy, you have happy chemicals running through your body. And when you are sad, you have sad chemicals in your body that can create tension and even pain, like an upset stomach or headaches. When something happens to you, your brain creates chemicals that make you react and feel emotions like fear or excitement.

Being aware of what's happening in your mind is an important part of feeling in control and managing your actions.

The first step to knowing your mind is to actually just be aware of your emotions.

Know

nAME MY FEELINGS

- - - - - - - - - - - -

Time Needed: **5 MINUTES**
Location: **ANYWHERE**

Sit comfortably. If you are comfortable, close your eyes.

Take a deep breath. In and out.

Now, just see what happens as you do nothing but breathe.

For example: You may feel tired and want to go to sleep. When you feel this, just say to yourself, "I feel tired."

You may start thinking about something that upset you at lunch. Just say to yourself, "I feel upset."

Your mind may wander to the birthday party you are supposed to go to this weekend. Just say to yourself, "I am excited."

Every time you notice a feeling, say, "I am [the feeling]."

And continue to breathe. In and out.

If your mind stays on that feeling, just feel it. But once it starts wandering and you feel something else, notice the new feeling.

After five minutes, you can take a deep breath and go on with your day.

This exercise helps you become aware of your feelings. Generally, your mind wanders from one thought and feeling to another; this is normal and natural. And, as you get to know your feelings better, you can learn how to make choices and do things to take better care of yourself.

> Create a list of your feelings. Keep adding to this list.
> Naming your feelings is really powerful!

Just Feel

What Your Mind Needs

· · · · ·

Just like you have to take care of your body to stay healthy, you also have to take care of your mind. Being mentally healthy means you feel like you can do what you need to do every day, are comfortable socially, can control your behavior, and can experience all your emotions without overwhelming anxiety. Of course, you may still get stressed, feel awkward at times, and become overwhelmed by your feelings! If you're mentally healthy, you just don't let your emotions control you; rather, you know your mind and your reactions and have ways to control them when you need to.

There are different components to having a healthy mind, many of which overlap with having a healthy body! The main components are:

- rest and relaxation

- movement

- mental activity
(like when you learn or focus)

- having fun

- connecting with others

Rest and Relaxation

In addition to regular sleep, your mind works well when it has quiet time to process information. In between the times you are learning and moving and playing and talking, if you give your mind quiet time, you will feel calmer, more energetic, and in control.

It can be really difficult to relax and give your mind down time, because the world has many ways to distract you! When your parents were kids, perhaps they spent time watching television or speaking on the phone with friends. Today, though, there are a million more things distracting your attention, especially the internet, online videos and video games, and social media.

Part of growing up and leading a healthy life is figuring out how to find the right balance between your distractions and giving your mind rest. Lots of adults haven't figured this out, so you'll be ahead of the game if you start to now!

Movement

When you exercise, your body releases good chemicals that make your mind healthier. Movement is critical to feeling good! Find a way to move every day, whether through sports, martial arts, running, or dance. Perhaps you can walk your dog or stretch in your house or do jumping jacks and sit-ups every day to get your body moving and your mind calmer and healthier.

Mental Activity

Learning new things and finding time to focus (such as studying or practicing a sport or instrument) are healthy habits for your mental health!

Your mind is a place full of endless magic that you can explore for your entire life. The more you use your mind, the healthier and more alert you will be as you grow older.

Think of facing a jungle full of trees, bushes, roots, puddles, and other unknown obstacles. There are so many hidden treasures to discover in this jungle! The first step is to slowly explore and learn about where you are. As you become more comfortable, you can clear a path to make it easier to make your way through what was once unknown.

You mind is like this—it is full of so many treasures, but you need to learn, explore, and focus to truly know it. When you focus, like when you are studying, your brain creates and strengthens the pathways inside that help you recall information, be informed, and make good choices.

Using all your senses—seeing, hearing, smelling, tasting, and touching—helps you keep your mind active. Reading, drawing, moving your body, talking to others, and listening also stimulate your brain in different ways.

Having Fun

Did you know that giggling, laughing, and just having fun make you healthier and happier? When you are with people who make you feel good or when you are doing something you enjoy or are just laughing, your mind releases happy chemicals into your body, which make you feel good. When you are having fun, your mind remembers these good experiences and you can even learn better. You may have fun in different ways—from being with friends to doing a puzzle to going to a concert to reading a good book. Whatever way you have fun is right for you.

Lots of adults often forget that life is also about fun and dreams and playing

freely! As a kid, you can play an important role in reminding your parents and teachers to laugh. You can also remind them how important it is for your health and development that you have downtime to play and laugh and just enjoy!

Connecting with Others

Some of us love being around lots of people and some of us prefer to be alone.

And, of course, on different days and at different times, you may prefer one or the other.

In general, having a few people you can connect with whom you can be yourself around with no pressure to perform or act a certain way can make you healthier and happier. This doesn't mean connecting just on social media; it means being with people in real time and face to face. Even connecting with one person can be incredibly powerful!

When you are physically with other people, you experience a range of emotions. Sometimes they are not always good ones, but that's all right. When you are with other people, you learn that your feelings change, which is normal and healthy.

You also become stronger by being around people, because you learn to deal with different emotions and situations in yourself, as well as recognizing that your friends might be experiencing a range of emotions, too.

How You Spend Your Time

· · · · ·

How you spend your time shapes who you are and who you will become.

You obviously spend time on some survival basics—sleeping, eating, and moving.

You probably also spend time learning at school, studying, and doing extracurricular activities.

Hopefully, you also have time to do things for fun, like hanging out with friends or family, or doing things alone like reading, drawing, playing video games or with toys, dancing, or just shooting hoops in the driveway or at the park.

Now ask yourself: do you have time to just be bored?

Letting your mind wander and having nothing to do sometimes is the best way to become more creative, to come up with new ways of doing things, or to just give your mind a much-needed rest. It's a great way to also check in with your mind and know how you feel.

Here is an exercise to help you to think about how you spend your time.

EXERCISE:

HOW DO I SPEND MY TIME?

- - - - - - - - - - - - -

Time Needed: **5 TO 10 MINUTES**
Location: **SOMEWHERE YOU CAN THINK**
Materials Needed: **PAPER, A PEN, AND
COLORED PENCILS OR CRAYONS**

On a piece of paper, draw a circle.

In the circle, write the words found below in the list. You can write them however you want. They can be organized around the circle or just written randomly:

- *Sleeping*

- *Eating*

- *Moving*

- *Learning/Studying/Practicing
  (Focus)*

- *Playing*

- *Friends*

- *Family*

- *Being bored*

Now, take a moment to think about how you spend your time. Also, note where you spend your time—at home, school, a local library, in your town, at a friend's house, or in nature?

With the crayons or colored pencils, color in the words according to how much of your time you think you spend on each one of these during the day. If you want to add colors to reflect the locations, as well, you may find this helpful.

Perhaps you spend more time sleeping than eating, and lots of time studying or practicing. Or, if you are on a sports team, maybe you spend more time moving and less time just being bored.

You will have a different-looking circle than your siblings, parents, and friends. But if you know your circle, you can decide if you feel good about it *and* want to make

some changes to achieve better balance in your life. Ask trusted adults for their feed-back, too. Thinking about how you can spend more time in nature, breathing fresh air, and being out in the sun can also help you feel good.

How You React to Things

· · · · ·

Imagine this scenario: You are in the car with your mom on your way to a birthday party, and there is a huge traffic jam. You are in the middle of the highway, and there is no way you will arrive at the party on time. You will probably be an hour late and miss half of the party.

Do you . . .

• get really upset and cry?

• hit something out of frustration?

• blame your mom?

• accept the situation for what it is?

• feel happy and relieved that you
have less time at the party?

• decide you just want to skip the party altogether?

• take advantage of the extra time you have with your mom?

• plan a special outing that you can do
with your friend at a future date?

All of the above are absolutely normal reactions to have and to feel in this situation. And each person probably will react and have different feelings in similar situations.

Some people, when they find themselves in stressful situations, get angry; some feel helpless; some accept things for what they are; and some think of new ways of doing things to try to relieve the stress or to solve a problem.

You may react to and feel differently about the same experience than your sibling or friend. Your body may also react differently from others. Some people may feel hot from frustration and anger; some may actually breathe easier because they feel relieved; or some may just freeze from uncertainty and fear about what will happen next.

When you start to notice how you feel in real and imaginary situations, you can start thinking ahead of time about how you would react next time if they actually did happen.

WHAT FRUSTRATES ME?

Time Needed: **5 MINUTES**
Location: **ANYWHERE**

Take a deep breath right now. In and out.

Think about something that really frustrates you:

- *Perhaps it is when you are running late for sports practice because your little sister wasn't ready.*

- *Or when you get a test back and got a lower grade than you thought.*

- *Or when a kid in your class raises their hand for every single question.*

- *Or when your parents say you have to go to a religious service in the morning and all you want to do is sleep in!*

As you think about what frustrates you, observe where in your body you are feeling this experience. Do you feel it in:

- *Your head?*
- *Your heart?*
- *Your throat?*

- *Your fists?*
- *Your stomach?*
- *Your whole body?*

Do you feel hot? Do you get stiff? What happens to your breath?

Now, take a deep breath, focusing on the part of your body in which you are feeling the frustration. Take an extra breath and remember that right now you are just thinking about how you react.

Think about one thing you can do next time you feel frustrated by this situation to make you feel better. Perhaps this is:

- *Taking a deep breath*
- *Moving around*
- *Saying something to yourself*
- *Using your words to express what you want to someone else*
- *Helping someone else*

Know

If you know the things that bother you in advance, you can prepare yourself (and others) to handle situations better. Also, as you feel tension rise in your body, you will recognize it. You can practice ways to slow down or cool your body and stop your body from overtaking you.

> Here's a cool-down exercise: Curl your tongue (or if you can't curl it, just keep it flat). Breathe in cool air through your open mouth. Close your mouth. Breathe out the hot air.

What Makes You Happy or Sad

· · · · ·

Different things make different people feel happy. It's the differences between people that makes you unique and the world more interesting.

You may be happiest sitting in your bed and reading a book.

You may be happiest when you are with your family during a holiday celebration.

Or when you are playing soccer outside with your friends.

You may be happiest when doing a group project in a classroom.

Or strategizing your next move during a chess game.

Or singing on stage in front of an audience.

Lots of things may make you happy, just like lots of things may make you feel sad and scared.

You may feel sad when you are at home with no one to play with.

Or when people you love are fighting.

Or when you do badly on a test.

Or when you have to do a group project.

Or when you are singing on stage in front of an audience.

Or when someone doesn't invite you to their birthday party.

Or if someone says something about you that you think is mean.

Life is about having a range of emotions. If you know generally what makes you feel happy and what makes you sad, you can start to shape your life a bit more. You may realize that sometimes when you are angry or annoyed, you are actually feeling sad or scared about something.

Here is an exercise to help you list what makes you happiest and what makes you sad.

WHAT MAKES ME HAPPY OR SAD?

Time Needed: **5 MINUTES**
Materials Needed: **PAPER AND PEN OR PENCIL**

On your piece of paper, write the following questions:

- *What makes me happy?*
- *What makes me sad?*

Write things, people, places, and activities under each one. Write as many different things that come to mind without thinking too much about it.

For things that make you happy, you could include things like food, clothes, your bed.

Or things you like to do like playing tennis, going to your dance class, walking your dog, or going to a movie (or maybe list specific movies). Or maybe there are people you like to be with like your cousin, best friend, or grandmother.

For things that make you sad, once again you can list things you don't like to do or people you prefer not to be around.

If you are uncomfortable or get emotional listing the sad things, skip this part of the exercise and choose instead to focus on only the things that make you happy.

Now that you have these two lists, you are more aware of what triggers you have that make you happy or sad.

You may want to share the sad list with an adult. However, if you aren't comfortable doing that, you can still feel more prepared for future situations that may make you upset because you have already recognized how they make you feel. You can even throw away the sad list if you don't want to keep it.

Keep the happy list somewhere safe where you can find it when you aren't feeling so great. It can be a reminder of what you can do or who you can reach out to when you need to brighten up your mood.

Where You Come From

· · · · ·

You come from somewhere and from other people.

When you were a baby, you probably had no idea or never thought about where you came from. But often, what happened when you were a baby can affect you later on in life.

As you grow older, you become more aware of the people and circumstances around you. You start to see how your background affects so many things about your life—from how much money your family has to your culture and neighborhood to the physical and mental health of your family or caretakers.

You may know your parents, your grandparents, and your extended family's story. Perhaps your family came from a different country, escaped a war, or traveled far to find a new home. Or maybe your family has lived where you live now for generations.

Some people do not know their parents or may be living separately from them. They may be unsure of physically where they came from, but if someone who is not their parent has loved them like a parent, they can know that they came from those caretakers, too.

Some people can look at where they came from with a lot of pride and joy. They can see how those who came before them were strong and creative and survived tough times.

Others may not know much or anything about their backgrounds. Or they may look at where they came from and see struggles, in extreme cases even addiction and violence. They may know that they don't want this to be part of their future.

Knowing about where you came from, even if it's hard to face at times, can help you eventually find strength to become who you want to be.

WHERE DO I COME FROM?

- - - - - - - - - -

Time Needed: **5 MINUTES**
Location: **A QUIET ROOM**

Find a place where you feel safe and at ease.

Sit comfortably.

Take a deep breath, and as you breathe in and out, reflect on how those who came before you also breathed air in and out.

Feel your body, scanning from your toes, up your legs, to your stomach and heart, stretching your fingers, and up into your face to the top of your head.

Reflect on how those before you also had bodies—and that your body is a continuation of their bodies and so many others that came before them.

Put your attention on your heart, and as you breathe in and out, see if you can feel your heart beating.

Reflect on how the hearts of those who came before you felt love and fear, sadness and excitement.

Breathe in and out.

As you feel the breath coming in and out, now knowing that those before you breathed, too, say to yourself, "I know I can always find my breath."

Knowing that you came from others, now feel your body as your own.

Scan your body from your toes up to your head, and say to yourself, "I will take care of my body the best I can."

Feel your heart beat, and honor all the emotions that those who came before you experienced. Know that you, too, will experience a range of emotions in this lifetime. Say to yourself, "I will honor my feelings."

Take another breath in and out.

Know

What Makes You Different
from Others

· ◦ ● ◦ ●

Every one of us is different.

We have different bodies. We come from different races. We look different on the outside.

We live in different places. Some of us live in cities or the suburbs, on farms, in the desert, by the ocean, or in the mountains.

Some of us may have experienced not having a place to live.

We have different religions and spiritual practices.

Some people have more money; others live with less. And some people struggle just to eat every day.

Our bodies work differently, and we react to situations differently.

Some of us like to be around lots of people and action, and some of us prefer to spend time alone and dislike crowded places.

We think about things differently.

The list of differences between each one of us goes on and on and on.

One of the keys to feeling good about your life is appreciating how you are unique.

You may have less or more than other people, but inside you can also find things that you feel good about in your life. You may not have the things that someone else has, but perhaps you have a friend you treasure who is truly special to you. Or you have a place you like to visit that makes you feel peaceful or joyful. Or perhaps you have a song you love or a talent you're proud of.

All of us feel like we are different from others at times, and that may make us feel alone, confused, and helpless. It's good to have a list of what makes you special as well as the same as others in times when you need to feel better.

Know

WHAT MAKES ME UNIQUE?

- - - - - - - - - - - - - - -

Time Needed: **5 MINUTES**
Location: **A QUIET ROOM, THE LIBRARY,
OR SOMEWHERE SAFE OUTSIDE**
Materials Needed: **A PAPER AND SOMETHING TO WRITE
OR DRAW WITH**

Sit comfortably in a place where you can think.

Take a deep breath. In and Out.

On your next breath, think I as you breathe in, and AM as you breathe out.

Again, I as you breathe in, and AM as you breathe out.

Now, think about three people in your life—perhaps a parent or sibling, a teacher, a friend, or someone you know through one of your activities.

On the piece of paper, write or draw three things that are the SAME between you and these three people.

It can be physical, like we each have a nose or have the same skin color.

Or it can be about something you do—we all eat or sleep.

Or it can be something more specific, like we all like the color red.

Now, think about three things that are DIFFERENT between you and these three people. (Choose three positive things for this exercise.)

It can be something physical about yourself that you like—perhaps the color of your hair or something you do differently from others or a talent you have.

After you put these on the page, take a moment to appreciate these things about yourself.

Realize that you share similarities to others, but that you also have unique things about you that you can celebrate.

You may want to keep adding to this list, putting it in a place to remind you about what makes you different (and special!) when you need it.

Take Responsibility

· · · · ·

One of the most important things you can learn early in your life is that taking responsibility for your feelings makes you powerful.

Think about these phrases:

- *I am responsible for what I see;*
- *I choose the feelings I experience;*
- *and I set the goals I will achieve.*

These words can be really annoying, because it can be really messy, scary, sad, and frustrating to take responsibility for your feelings when you are going through hard times. For example, think about the following and answer if you think you are responsible if:

- someone that you thought was your friend didn't invite you to his birthday party?
- your little sister was being a pest, bugging you when you were trying to study for a test, and you didn't do well?
- there is a bully who is harassing you at school or online?
- your parents are getting divorced?
- your cousin has cancer and is suffering?

Things happen sometimes that we cannot control, and life can be really tough. Really, really tough. And no, you are not always responsible when bad things happen to you or others. Not at all. There are lots of twists and turns in life, as well as things in your family, community, or the world that you will never be able to control.

But you have the power inside of you to see things more clearly, to embrace your feelings (which include anger and fear), and to take action that may make your life and those of the people around you easier.

In most situations, your reactions, your feelings, and your body's responses are automatic at first. The fight-or-flight-or-freeze response that is part of being a human is that you want to angrily fight back, run away, or just freeze with fear.

However, part of being a human being is that you can pause, reflect on situations, control how you react, and make choices.

Just Feel

You may be able to see some things from another perspective, and even taking a deep breath can influence your reactions and actions. Think of the scenarios from earlier in this section. Now think about how you could react to those if you took a deep breath and thought about things from another's perspective:

- Instead of only feeling hurt by not being invited to the party (and it is okay and normal to feel hurt), you could also think about what you could do to make your friends know they matter to you.

- You could create stricter rules for your siblings at study time, and ask your parents to help enforce the rules.

- If you aren't feeling safe because of that bully at school, perhaps you can try to talk to a teacher or adult about how they can protect you better and how you can avoid the bully.

Then, there are things you can't control—like your cousin getting a disease or that your parents are going through a difficult time. But you still can decide to check in with your cousin and spend time with them or write them a note, or support your parents by telling them good things about your day and making them smile about something you did. You can also support yourself by doing things that will help you feel better, too, like talking to someone about your feelings, taking some personal quiet time in nature, writing in a journal, or doing something physical to help take away some of your stress.

Embrace Your Feelings

• • • • •

A person's basic feelings include fear, anger, sadness, happiness, calm, and excitement.

Every one of us feels these emotions in our life. You can't stop your feelings; they are automatic and part of being human.

Your body reacts first to feelings—you literally can feel your body heat up when you get angry; your stomach might feel butterflies when you are scared; your heart beats faster when you are excited; your hands may get tingly when you are joyful; and your eyes could well with tears when you are sad.

As your body reacts to feelings, your mind interprets what happened and makes you feel stressed, anxious, guilty, happy, or joyful. You can't necessarily control these things.

Choose

You *do* have the ability to control your feelings from taking over your life, though. This control is important, because otherwise, when you get angry, you may just want to hit someone, or when you are scared, you may do something that you regret later.

In a moment when you feel scared or angry, you can:

* pause
* pay attention to what you are feeling
* name your feeling
* take a deep breath
* and make a choice about the best way to respond

By naming your feelings, you help your mind take over the physical reactions in your body, and then you can have more control over how you react to those feelings.

> Another way to pause in a stressful situation is to STOP. Here is what that means: S: Stop. T: Take a deep breath. O: Observe what's happening in your body. P: Proceed.

EXERCISE:
FEELING MY FEELINGS

- - - - - - - - - -

Time Needed: **LESS THAN 1 MINUTE**
Location: **ANYWHERE**

In this exercise, you are going to set some strategies for the next time you have overwhelming feelings.

You can do this exercise alone with your eyes open or closed. Or you can choose to do this exercise along with a trusted adult or mentor.

Sit comfortably.

Take a deep breath. Breathe in and breathe out.

Take another breath. In and out.

Think about what your body feels like when you are angry.

Without judgement, think about where and how you feel anger in your body.

Take a breath, in and out.

Now, complete this sentence: "Next time I feel angry, I will feel my body, say that I feel angry, and take a deep breath. Then I will say, 'I can choose how I respond to this anger.'"

Think of a time you recently got angry. Reflect on how you reacted. Now, think about another way you could have acted.

Repeat the process above for when you feel sad and when you feel scared.

Choose Your Words

· · · · ·

Your words—to yourself and to others—are incredibly powerful. Every day, and every moment of the day, you can choose how you speak and how your words affect your feelings.

You can choose to tell yourself that you don't like your body, that you aren't smart enough, or that you don't have enough friends. But if that's what you keep saying, then you probably aren't going to feel that great about yourself.

You can also choose to tell yourself that you are going to make healthier choices about what you eat and how much you move, that you are going to connect with a friend or sibling today by really listening to them, and that you are going to do something for your mind that makes you feel smart and happy (even if it isn't school-work). When you give yourself positive talk, then you will start to see how your words influence your feelings.

Your words also influence those around you. Have you noticed that when someone is in a bad mood and complains or criticizes, you don't feel so great? Or if you are rude to your teacher or a parent, they aren't as nice to you as they may be when you speak kindly?

What you give is often what you get back. Begin to play around with your words—to yourself and to others—and see how they change your feelings. An *affirmation* is a word or phrase that you say to yourself or share with others that motivates you and makes you feel good. Affirmations can help you stay focused and look at situations with a different attitude.

USE KIND WORDS TODAY

Time Needed: **1 DAY**
Location: **EVERYWHERE YOU GO TODAY**
Materials needed: **NOTECARDS OR
A PIECE OF PAPER, A PEN, OR PENCIL**

Decide that today you are going to use positive words and that you will approach people with a smile and kind attitude.

Spend the day saying "Good Morning," "Please," "Thank You," and use other nice words as you speak to people throughout one day.

When speaking with someone, think about how you can use a kind tone of voice, and consider a way to give them an honest compliment.

At the beginning of the day, you may want to write affirmations to remind you how you want to feel. You may write things like:

- *Remember to smile when speaking today.*

- *Say "please" and "thank you" today.*

- *Ask someone how they feel today.*

- *Give someone an honest compliment today.*

At the end of the day, before you go to sleep, look at your affirmations and think about how you may or may not have achieved them. Think about how you felt when you spoke kindly. Did the people around you seem at all different today? Do you think your words affected their moods?

Was it difficult to be kinder than usual or did it feel natural? Do you think you need to practice the skills above?

Choose

Choose to Listen

· · · · ·

There is a difference between hearing and listening.

We hear noises around us—the noise of a fan in our room, the buzzing of a light, the doorbell. We hear voices and chatter, coughs and laughs, and words from those around us. Our ears help us hear, taking in the sounds from around us and helping our brain process the information.

When we listen, however, we use our body *and* our mind, and we feel the responses to the sounds.

When you listen to your friend tell you about something that made her feel really happy, can you feel her excitement? When you listen, you feel the tone of her voice, the twinkle in her eyes, and what her body is telling you without words. By listening, you feel connected to her story.

Listening helps you understand other people better as well as learn how to connect with them in a more meaningful way. Good leaders are often good listeners, too. They learn how to hear more than just the words people say to them. They also observe what makes others excited, what makes them feel good or nervous about themselves, and then interact with them in a way that makes them feel heard and supported.

> When you listen to music that you love, do you feel something inside—
> perhaps joy or excitement or sadness? What other things do you
> listen to that influence your feelings?

Choose

EXERCISE:

TELL ME A STORY

- - - - - - - - - -

Time Needed: **KEEP IT FLEXIBLE**
Location: **A PLACE WHERE YOU CAN FREELY INTERACT
WITH ANOTHER PERSON**

For this exercise, ask someone you love to tell you a story about something that made them really happy. Maybe they'll tell you about the time they did something they were really proud of, met someone they knew they would love (perhaps you!), or experienced a very special moment.

As you listen to them, don't worry about the time. Instead, listen to them with every part of your body, and try to experience what they are telling you as if you were with them while they are going through this for the first time. Soak in the colors and smells and sounds they describe. Imagine the other people who may be part of their story.

Look at the expressions on their face. Notice their body language—many people tell stories with their hands and use their whole bodies.

As they tell their story, imagine the scenes they describe and try to feel what they are remembering.

Feel how your heart feels as they smile. When they laugh, do you feel different?

Does it feel like they are feeling those same emotions now? Do you feel any emotions as you listen to their story?

When they are done telling their story, thank them for sharing this special moment with you.

Feel What Another Feels

• • • • •

As you pay attention to listening to others and learn to be open to their feelings, you will also learn how to be comfortable feeling what others feel.

If they are sad about something that is happening in their life, you, too, may also feel sad. As they share a struggle they may be facing, you may also feel what it is like to be in their position.

Empathy describes when you feel what someone else is feeling. Empathy allows you to be more aware of other people's feelings and why they may do the things they do. When you are empathetic, you are more understanding and take things that happen to you less personally. So, when your friend unexpectedly gets frustrated with you, you realize that they are upset about something else and are just taking it out on you. When you are empathetic, you show other people that you are someone they can turn to when they need help.

When someone is telling you about something they want to share—happy or sad—give them your whole attention. Turn off the television or stop the video game you may be playing, and don't check your phone. Rather, listen to them with your whole heart and body.

Believe it or not, many times you don't even need to do anything to help someone who is having a problem. Just listening and being present can truly help them.

Similarly, when you are in a situation where people may be upset or arguing, you can pay attention to the things happening outside of the words and voices you are hearing. You can learn a lot from body language, how people are positioned in the room, and the tone of their voices. Being an empathetic person can help you guide others to resolve conflict. You can also gain confidence by being a person who knows how to read others' feelings well.

Some people are so sensitive and empathetic to others that it can create more stress for them. If you find that you easily get involved in other people's struggles, you may not want to spend too much time getting involved in their experiences. You can be honest with them about how their emotions affect you. Try to determine how best you can be a good friend or family member while setting limits that feel right to you.

FEEL WHAT SOMEONE ELSE FEELS

- - - - - - - - - - -

Time Needed: **KEEP IT FLEXIBLE**
Location: **SOMEWHERE YOU CAN LISTEN AND SPEAK FREELY**

You should do this exercise with a trusted adult—like a parent, teacher, or caretaker.

Ask a trusted adult to tell you a story about a task that was difficult for them to accomplish at one point in their life. Perhaps it was a time when they struggled in school or at work, when they thought they failed at something, or when they had a difficult time with a friend.

Listen to their story. Try not to interrupt them with comments, but just listen without asking any questions.

Once they are done telling you their story, ask if you can repeat the story to them (to make sure you heard the story how they meant to tell it), and then reflect out loud with them on how they felt at the time.

This exercise is helpful for you to learn that others have gone through difficult times, just like you. It also shows you that everyone fails or struggles at times, but that people can get through challenges and learn from past experiences. This exercise also helps you get better at listening because you repeat the story to them!

> When listening or talking to someone else, make sure you are looking at them. Eye contact helps you connect with and understand others better.

Say "I'm Sorry"

• • • • •

When you do something wrong, do you take responsibility for your actions, or do you try to pretend like you didn't do anything that needs apologizing for?

When people make mistakes, often the first feeling they experience is fear. Fear can lead to lying, blaming others, feeling guilty, and making new mistakes to cover up the original one.

Fear also leads to stress—confusion in your mind and tension in your body. When

Choose

you have stress, it's harder to sleep, focus, and generally feel energetic or happy.

Everyone makes mistakes. We are all human, and no one is perfect. The world would be really boring if we were all robots who acted the same and never made mistakes. Mistakes can help us learn and become the person we aim to be.

There are two types of mistakes: small mistakes and big mistakes.

Small mistakes usually don't affect other people, but rather give you an opportunity to learn. Think of homework and tests that you take at school—the point of assessments is to help you set a guideline to study, but you most likely make mistakes and need to make corrections. This is how you learn what you need to focus on more to be successful. Similarly, your sports coach or piano teacher gives you advice or constructive criticism on how you can improve doing something you love to do so you can become even better at it than you currently are.

Then, there are mistakes that affect other people—the big mistakes. When you say something that hurts another person or puts someone in a difficult or dangerous position, taking responsibility will make you feel better in the long run.

While admitting you are wrong and saying sorry is often the hardest and scariest thing to do, you will find that once you take responsibility for your actions or for your mistakes, your body and mind can begin to move on.

Learning to say sorry when you have made a mistake is a big part of taking responsibility and feeling good about yourself. You may also learn that when you say sorry and take responsibility, others actually see you in a new light. They know you are someone they will be able to trust in the future and may give you more chances in the future or even more respect.

Forgive Others

● ● ● ●

When you are hurt by someone else, you may feel angry, alone, or sad.

Forgiving people who hurt you often feels wrong or difficult, because you feel they don't deserve it. But, by holding onto the anger you are feeling, you are actually continuing to feel the pain inside for a longer period of time. Hurt and pain can also have physical effects that make you feel tired or sick or depressed.

Forgiving someone else does not mean they're right. It also doesn't mean that you need to justify anything or say sorry (unless, deep down inside, you think you did something wrong and then you can take responsibility, too). Forgiving others also doesn't mean that you still need to interact with them. It just means that you decide that you're not going to let their actions affect your mind any longer than necessary.

You can't force someone else to admit they're wrong or say sorry to you. Sometimes, you may also be upset with someone for hurting you and they don't even know how you are feeling. Part of resolving conflict is also sharing your feelings in an honest way, without forcing the other person to admit they're wrong. You can usually do this best once you have paused and reflected on what happened and how it made you feel.

Here are some basic steps to help you forgive:

• Separate yourself from the situation that created tension.
This may mean you take a break from a friend or tell your sibling
or parent you need time alone to think.

• Replay in your mind the situation that upset you and see if
you can understand it from the other person's perspective.

• Ask yourself if you are making assumptions about what happened.

• If you are comfortable, find a safe time and place to ask the other person
why they did whatever they did to upset you.

• Determine if you agree or disagree with their response.

• Tell them honestly how you feel and that you are hurt.

• Be open to an apology from the person who hurt you.

• If they apologize, and you believe them, forgive and move on.
(Don't force them to apologize, because you know it won't be an honest one.)

• If they don't apologize, know that you expressed how you felt and move on.

• It is best to talk directly to a person who has hurt you.
Avoid texting or sending messages on social media, because messages
can be misinterpreted when they are read.

When someone has hurt your feelings, usually it is best to resolve the conflict directly with that person. However, if someone has *physically* hurt you, then you need to turn to a trusted adult, teacher, counselor, or social worker to help you. It is always okay to ask someone else for help. If you are unsure, it is always best to check in with a trusted adult who can help you think through the best approach for you and to perhaps even help you figure out what to do next. And, there are definitely times when you can forgive a person who has hurt you without speaking to them directly—you simply forgive them in your heart and then work to move on.

WHY AM I HURTING?

- - - - - - - - - - - - - - -

Time Needed: **2 MINUTES**

Location: **A QUIET PLACE WHERE YOU CAN THINK**

If you are hurting because someone hurt you, being clear about your feelings is an important step.

Sometimes your feelings can be overwhelming, so it is good to try this exercise with someone you love and trust whom you can explore your feelings with.

If you feel hurt by someone, think about what exactly they did to make you feel that way.

Separate what you think they did and your feelings from their actual actions. For example, instead of saying "My mom made me feel guilty," say, "My mom asked me to clean my room." State the facts, not what you thought they did or said. What words did they actually use? Who else was there, and would that person agree with what you think happened?

If you still feel that they did something wrong, know that your feelings are true for you.

Try to see if you can understand why they may have acted the way they did. You may not agree with them, but see if you can understand their point of view. Talk through your ideas with your trusted adult.

See if you can express your feelings without just blaming the other person. Finish this sentence using facts for their actions: I felt _____ (sad, angry, hurt) because when you _____ (state the actual action they did), I felt _____ (scared, lonely, etc.).

With your trusted adult, decide if you think you can talk to the person who hurt you and tell them how you feel. Do not expect an apology from them; rather, focus on how you have power over the situation by expressing your feelings.

If it is not safe or comfortable to talk to them (and this may be the case), or if now is not the right time, don't approach them right away. Instead, decide that you know your feelings, you know you are right, and let your feelings go. You can do this by talking to your trusted adult. You could also try to write down your feelings on a piece of paper and then tear it

Choose

up and throw it away. Or you could feel the hurt in your body and breathe in new energy with fresh air then blow out those feelings. You may also choose to focus on the positive feelings you get from people with whom you feel safe.

Learn from Your Experiences

• • • • •

Your life may be full of things you have to do: homework, quizzes, and tests at school, physical goals for sports, or a piece of music you need to learn for your performance, to name a few. As you grow older, you will most likely keep adding things that you have to do to prove that you are learning and developing the way that your school, coaches, and society want you to.

It may feel awful when you get a bad grade on your math test or don't make the minimum sit-ups on your PE test. And sometimes, even if you try to do better, it still remains hard.

Have faith that all these challenges are a part of learning and making you a stronger person. The greatest athletes in the world did not win every game they played; rather, they understood that they could learn from mistakes. Great scientific discoveries were often made by one experiment not working and then the scientist trying something different and stumbling on an answer by mistake.

Think of this scenario: You just got a really low grade on a math test. How do you react?

You may tell yourself that you are really bad at math and give up. You accept that you will never be good at math. This mindset is letting a small misstep stop you from reaching your potential.

You can approach a low grade (or any challenge) in a different way.

You can ask yourself the following questions:

• Did I understand the problems that we learned in class?

• Did I honestly do my homework and study for the test?

• Did my teacher do a good job of explaining the material?

You can go back to your mistakes and understand why you made them. You can ask your teacher to review the material again with you. Or, if that doesn't feel right, you can ask a parent or classmate for help. You can also ask a librarian to help you find an online site to help you understand the math better.

You can think of new ways to study—perhaps with a classmate or adult, instead of just alone. You can also reflect on other things that may have affected you. There are days you don't feel well or when something stressful happened at home—they may seem unrelated but can affect you. Think about your body's and mind's health: did you sleep and eat enough before you went to school that day?

Reflecting on your experiences, and especially learning from ones that didn't go so well, are important ways to become stronger, happier, and more successful so that you can feel like you can achieve your personal best.

It is also important to remember that sometimes things are beyond your control. Everyone makes mistakes, everyone feels like they have failed (often many, many times). But those who end up doing well learn, ask for help, and try again.

Try, and Try, and Try. Again, and Again, and Again!

• • • • •

Do you have any memories of what it was like when you started walking?

It's worth watching a baby who is learning to walk. They begin by reaching, maybe crawling. Some slide from side to side, or roll over and over, or come up with a new move no one has seen before.

Then, most babies begin to pull themselves up, perhaps on a piece of furniture or with the help of someone else.

And then they fall.

Often, if you watch a baby tumble, they fall on their bottom or their face. Maybe they cry for a few seconds, or maybe they giggle.

But the amazing thing is that most babies will try to get up again. They will fall, but they will also get back up and try doing it again.

When you get older and smarter, you may forget that, as a toddler, before you were able to do most things, you had to try, and try, and try. Again, and again, and again.

Even though you had to keep trying, you didn't spend too much time thinking about how difficult it was to stand up and balance or that it could be embarrassing when you fell down.

For some reason, though, perhaps as you are getting older, when you stumble over something, you get nervous or embarrassed. You decide that maybe it is not worth trying to do it again, and you convince yourself you don't really care even though, deep down inside, maybe you still do.

This is all normal—it is part of becoming more responsible and making good decisions.

But, once in a while, bring back that baby energy and remember how good it felt, after all that effort and the trying and falling, to make that first walk across the room!

How about taking a moment to twirl around and around or to crawl on the ground like you are a baby again? Let go, laugh, and just be silly!

When to Let Go

• • • • •

Giving up is different than letting go.

While sometimes you need to try and try and try again to achieve something that is important to you, other times you will know inside that it is time to move on and let go. This is for things you do but also sometimes for relationships, too.

There is a story in Greek mythology of Sisyphus pushing a rock up a hill. Every time he was almost at the top, the rock would fall and he would have to start it all over again. He spent his entire life pushing that rock up the hill! At some point, Sisyphus needed to see that he could achieve more by doing something else with his time!

Letting go of a hobby or a project can be hard because it can feel like you failed. Perhaps you have played soccer your whole life, and you are actually good at it, but you really dread playing the sport. You are scared that you will disappoint your coach or your parents if you tell them you don't want to play anymore. If you can find the courage to tell them the truth, you may be surprised how supportive they are because you took the responsibility on yourself to make a decision.

Sometimes, people in your life are not nice to you, like other kids at school who don't include you in their groups. But you are scared to stop trying to make them like you or be your friend. And the idea of letting go is just too scary, because you fear that you will be alone. But, once you let go, you may find you are happier than ever before and you may even discover new friends or hobbies.

Finding ways to know when something doesn't feel right anymore is a really important skill that will help you become stronger, more successful, and happier in your life.

DO I LIKE THIS?

- - - - - - - - - -

Time Needed: **A FEW SECONDS BEFORE, DURING, AND AFTER AN ACTIVITY**

Ask yourself before you head out to do one of your activities, "Am I excited to do this?"

As you are doing the activity, ask yourself, "Does this feel good and make me happy?"

After you do something, ask yourself, "Did that feel good?"

A week from now, ask yourself, "Am I glad I did that?"

If it all doesn't feel good, ask yourself, "Why am I doing this?" There are some things you know you need to do because they are good for you (like going to school and studying), but there are also things you do because you've chosen to do them.

There could be a good reason that you are still pursuing something that you don't like and that you can't let go of. But knowing the reason why will always be helpful and will empower you more. Like sometimes a crazy workout can be hard and difficult, but you know in the long run you will feel great.

There is no need to make immediate decisions about implementing changes in your life, but keep talking to the adults you trust to make sure you are on the right path and are doing things that make you feel both happy and healthy.

Choose

Choose Your Friends, Mentors, and Heroes

* * * * *

Did you know research has shown that if you have a happy friend, you are more likely to be happy? Who you surround yourself with and look up to influence who you are and who you will become.

You may feel like you don't have enough friends or that you want to be part of a group that doesn't include you. But you should strive only to be part of groups where you can be yourself, where you respect the others, and where you are treated with kindness.

Also, it is important to remember that having *one* good friend can make you happier and feel more connected than being part of a larger social group. Seek out real, meaningful relationships in which you feel good about yourself rather than ones in which you are trying to be someone you are not.

Similarly, if you're going to be on social media, it's important that you're proud of how you present yourself to the world. Having more followers or more likes doesn't mean you're liked more—in fact, for some people, becoming addicted to other people's approval can make them feel really lonely. Social media can make you feel *more* left out because other people create stories they want to make them feel better about themselves, but often those stories don't represent what they are doing on a regular basis or how they really feel all the time.

Seeking out mentors—older kids and adults—whom you respect can also change your life. Having someone to approach for advice, share problems with, and celebrate successes helps you feel connected and good about yourself.

Last, but not least, finding real-life heroes and role models can help you strive to be your best self. These may be people you don't even know but whom you admire because of how hard they work, how they want to serve, how they have kept going even when things are tough, and how they have given back to the world.

EXERCISE:
WHOM DO I WANT TO BE AROUND?

- - - - - - - - - - - -

Time Needed: **5 MINUTES**
Location: **A QUIET PLACE**

Before you begin this exercise, just pause a minute to quiet down. Take a deep breath, in and out. And then take two more breaths.

Breathe in. Pause. Breathe out. Breathe in. Pause. Breathe out.

In this exercise, you are going to set an intent about how and with whom you want to spend your time. An intent is your deep desire. It represents the kind of person you want to be and the kind of actions you want to take.

Think of one person who is a friend or who you think would be a good friend. Set an intention to be a good friend to this person. Take a deep breath, in and out. Right now you don't have to worry about how you can be a good friend, just tell yourself that you want to be one.

Think of one person—an older kid or adult—who you think would be a good mentor to you. Set an intention to get to know this person better.

Think of a real-life hero or role model. This may be someone you don't know but whom you admire. Set an intention to learn more about this person and the qualities that you admire in them.

An intent is like planting a seed deep down inside of you. Once you know you want to feel something, you'll start figuring out how to make it happen!

Sit Straight and Stand Tall

• • • • •

Do you notice how when you sit or stand or move in different ways you feel differently?

Your posture and movement can reflect how you are feeling inside, but choosing to move in different ways can also shape your feelings. Having good posture also helps energy move through your body in a more natural way and automatically makes you feel better!

When you look at these pictures, do you make a judgement about how these kids are feeling?

The way we present our bodies tells others a lot about how we are feeling.

Noticing how you use your body can help you have more control over your own feelings.

SIT AND STAND TALL

- - - - - - - - - - - -

Time Needed: **2 TO 3 MINUTES**
Location: **WHEREVER YOU ARE RIGHT NOW**

Right now, as you are reading this, take a moment to notice your body.

Perhaps you are sitting or lying down. Before you do anything, just notice how your body is feeling in this position.

Notice if you slouch while sitting or if you sit upright.

Where are your legs—leaning up on something, on the ground, or straight in front of you?

How are you holding this book (or if you are listening, in what position do you listen)?

Take a deep breath.

And, if you can, choose right now to sit in a strong, upright position.

Put your feet on the ground.

Pull back your shoulders, and imagine a string pulling the top of your head up to the sky so you straighten your back.

Breathe deep again.

Put this book down for a moment, and put your hands on your lap.

Notice what it feels like when you are sitting up straight and taking a deep breath.

Do you feel any different?

Now try the same thing standing up.

Stand up straight, your hips slightly apart and your feet on the ground.

Let your arms hang naturally at your sides, your head raised high like it's being suspended from a string, and make sure your neck is straight.

Look forward with your eyes and take a deep breath, in and out.

When you sit or stand tall, you feel stronger and more in control. Throughout each day, notice how you are sitting or standing and adjust your position. How you sit or stand affects your mood. When you are conscious of your posture and work to sit or stand taller, you will be more alert and more energetic.

> Standing straight and tall and taking a deep breath is called Mountain Pose. Imagine you are a mountain climbing high into the sky. The clouds are around and below you, but you are strong and stable.

Feel Pride and Joy

· · · · ·

It is important to feel proud of yourself when you have accomplished something great or when you have tried your best at something. Also, it's important to embrace joy when you're happy. You can feel pride and joy in your body when you are experiencing it.

Good hormones flow through you when you have accomplished something or when you have connected with someone you love.

When you're in this good state of mind, you can use your breath to let the feelings seep in and affect your feelings of happiness and contentment. Positive and empowering feelings help your body and brain feel good and healthy. They help your immunity (how you fight off disease) and make you stronger when challenges come your way.

BREATHE IN PROUD FEELINGS

Time Needed: **5 MINUTES**
Location: **SOMEWHERE QUIET AND COMFORTABLE**

Think of a time when you felt proud of yourself.

It may be a time you were kind to someone else, when you accomplished something you felt good about, or when you know you tried your best.

Now, imagine your favorite color.

Take a conscious deep breath, and as you breathe in, see that color coming into your body and spreading through every part of it.

Feel the pride and your color going into every cell inside of you.

Breathe out.

Take another breath in. See the color go inside you again, and as you breathe out, imagine how your color spreads with your breath, creating a color around you.

Breathe in and out.

Next time you feel proud of something you are doing, try to remember to breathe in your pride, associating it with your favorite color. Let that pride seep into every fiber of your being!

> At the end of the day, think about three things you are grateful for.
> It's a great way to get you in a good mood before going to sleep!

TAKE ACTION

Feel Your Body

. . . . .

Certain parts of your body may be more sensitive to feeling particular emotions. For example, some people feel butterflies in their stomach when they are scared, or their throat feels tight when they are nervous about speaking in front of a large group of people. Some people feel tingling in their hands when they are excited or feel heart ache when they are sad.

One way to connect emotions and your body is to focus on how different parts of your body carry your feelings.

1. As you travel up your spine, you may notice that different areas hold more pressure when you're feeling stressed.

2. At the bottom of your back, near your butt, is where you may carry feelings of safety. When you feel taken care of and that you have what you need to survive, you feel confident and fearless and can sit tall. However, sometimes when you are scared or anxious, your bathroom routine can be unsettled— you either can't go or things are loose down there!

3. Below your belly button is often an area where you feel excitement. It is also considered the area for creativity, linked to where a mom carries her baby.

4. Around your stomach is where you feel power. It is also where you feel a lot of your stress—butterflies in your stomach or your breathing getting faster when you are nervous or scared.

5. Your heart is where you feel love and connection. This is why when you are with someone you love, your heart feels like it is bursting with joy, or when someone hurts you, you feel heartbroken.

6. In your throat and neck is where you feel good about what you have to say in the world and how you communicate. Often, if you are feeling like no one hears or understands you, your throat may get dry and it feels like you can't talk.

7. Between your eyebrows is often where your energy goes when you are making an important decision. Do you notice how your eyebrows sometimes raise or you feel pressure in that area when you are thinking hard? When you doubt yourself or don't trust someone or a situation, you may feel pressure in this area and get a headache.

8. Finally, the top of your head is where you may feel connected to something bigger than yourself. Think about the space above your head—feel the space between your head and the roof that may be above you, past the clouds in the sky, and up into the galaxy.

Here is an exercise to help you become more familiar with the different energy centers of your body. For this exercise, you will use the colors of the rainbow to open up these areas inside you.

Take Action

FEELING MY BODY WITH COLOR

- - - - - - - - -

Time Needed: **5 TO 10 MINUTES**
Location: **SOMEWHERE COMFORTABLE**

Sit comfortably, and take a deep breath.

Close your eyes, and take another deep breath, in and out. In and Out.

Let's focus on the different energy points in your body, and breathe in and out the various colors below. You will be using the colors of the rainbow, as this is an easy way to remember the order. However, if you connect to your body with different colors, or even the same one, that works, too! If you feel like one area is really calling out to you, feel free to pause and breathe into that area of your body.

Let go and have fun with this exercise. Being open to trying something new is a great way to learn and just have fun.

- *Put your attention on where your butt touches the chair beneath you. Take a deep breath and envision red air swirling in that area.*

- *Move to the area below your belly button, imagining the color orange warming you.*

- *Shift to your stomach and lungs, breathing in yellow air. In and out.*

- *As you move to your heart, feel the color green.*

- *Put your attention on your throat, and envision a light blue color.*

- *As you shift up to the space between your eyebrows, let that blue turn darker until it is a rich, dark blue.*

- *Now, put your attention on the top of your head, and imagine the space between your head and the roof above you. Think about the space beyond the roof, going way up high into the sky and the universe above. As you breathe in and out, imagine the color purple.*

Before you open your eyes, feel if one of the energy centers wants more focus. Take a deep breath in and out, nurturing it with the air around you. You may choose to stick with the colors of the rainbow or you may choose to mix it up a bit. Whatever you decide to do is okay. You can't do anything wrong here—just feel your body by being aware of it.

Once you are ready, gently open your eyes.

Move into Your Feelings

• • • • •

Moving into feelings can help you shift your mood. When you need more power, you can use your body to feel power. When you need rest, you can move your body to feel rest. There are different ways to physically change your mood!

Perhaps you are feeling a little unstable—like too many things are happening around you and you are floating and uneasy. Imagine a majestic tree standing tall. The tree has strength and grace and seems like it can weather the most difficult storm. Imagine yourself like this tree. By standing tall, by taking a deep breath, you can decide that you, too, can weather any storm.

Or perhaps there are times when you just need a break. You may feel sad or like you have too much to do and want to lie down or take time away from the chaos in your head. Lying down and giving your body rest is a good way to honor what you may be feeling.

At other times you may feel like you need to loosen up, to be silly, and even to roll around on the ground. Shaking your body out, swaying back and forth, or wiggling your arms and legs like loose noodles can help you feel good!

Sometimes when you are focusing for a long time, just getting up and doing ten jumping jacks can give you more energy. Or take a quick break and go for a walk outside and breathe in fresh air.

Some people may find that they can process their feelings through dance or martial arts or by going for a run. You can try different things to see what feels best for you. You may also find that mixing up different activities helps the most.

Experiment with various ways you can move to change how you are feeling. The great thing about your body is that *you* control it. You can use movement to get more energy or to slow down to change how you are feeling.

Just Feel

Tree Pose

Feeling balanced inside means you are calm, steady, and strong. It means you can breathe easily and see clearly in this very moment.

When you want to feel balanced, you can try Tree Pose. This pose requires you to balance on each side of your body, to use your breath to get that balance, and to calm your mind to stand still.

Stand tall with your hands at your sides.

Take a deep breath. Breathe in—pause—breathe out.

Put your hands together in front of your body.

Keep your right foot on the ground, and slowly lift your left foot. Find your balance. You can keep your left foot by your ankle, right above your knee, or folded up at the top of your leg.

Breathe in and focus on balancing.

When you find that point of balance, breathe in and out.

Put your left foot down.

Take a deep breath. In and Out.

Now, keep your left foot on the ground, and slowly lift your right foot. Find your balance, placing your right foot wherever is most comfortable on your left leg.

Breathe in and out when you find that point of balance.

Put your right foot down.

With both feet back on the ground, breathe in and out.

Happy Baby

Babies are really good at expressing their feelings. When they are hungry, have wet diapers, are uncomfortable, or are scared, they cry. When they are sleepy, they rub their eyes and fall asleep.

And, when they are happy, they kick their legs, wave their arms, and roll from side to side as they giggle and gurgle and smile. You, too, can feel like a happy baby in this pose.

Lie on your back.

Bend your knees, holding them with your hands.

With your left hand on your left knee or foot and your right hand on your right knee or foot, start to separate your legs from each other.

Roll from side to side, massaging your lower back.

You can play around with opening your legs and closing them.

Remember what it felt like to be a baby and just roll around and have fun.

Bring your knees back together and hug them into your body.

Put your feet down and rest for a moment.

Breathe in and out.

Child's Pose

This pose is a great one to do when you just want to relax, to clear your mind, and to take a break from the craziness around you. Sometimes when you get really upset and know your body reacted without your control, this pose can help you settle down.

Kneel on your legs, with your knees and the tops of your feet on the ground, keeping your feet under you with your big toes touching.

Find a position that is most comfortable for you where you will be able to bend forward. This may mean you keep your knees spread apart so your head can fit between your knees. For some people, kneeling may be hard so you can also just sit cross-legged or in another position that lets you bend forward.

Bend forward and put your forehead in between your knees.

Keep your arms by your side and take a deep breath, in and out.

Now, stretch your arms forward in front of you and keep your palms on the ground.

Take a few deep breaths. In and out. In and out. In and out.

Bring your arms to your sides again, and take another breath, in and out.

Raise your chest and move into a regular seated position.

Take another breath, in and out.

Warrior Pose

This pose gives you the inner strength to take on any challenge. By doing this pose, you'll feel like a warrior who is stable, just, and ready to strike only if needed.

Begin by standing tall and strong. Your feet should be on the ground hip distance apart. Your arms will be dangling at your sides. Your head should be straight, like it's being pulled up to the sky by an invisible string.

Turn to your right, and move your right foot away from your left foot.

As you move, stretch your arms to opposite sides of the room.

Find your balance as your left foot turns slightly to the right side (at a 45-degree angle), and the other foot turns completely to the right side.

Bend your right knee so that it comes over your right foot.

Keep your hands stretching in a strong line, imagining the energy going from your fingers to each wall.

Only lean forward as much as is comfortable for you, and not too much into your knee. Focus your energy on being stable in the middle of your body.

Take a deep breath.

Now slowly come back to facing forward, standing straight and tall.

Time for the other side.

Turn to your left, and move your left foot away from your right.

As you move, stretch your arms to opposite sides.

Find your balance as your right foot slightly turns to the left side, and the other foot turns completely to the left side.

Bend your left knee so that it comes over your left foot. Remember to focus the energy on being stable in the middle of your body.

Keep your hands stretching in a strong line.

Take a deep breath.

Come slowly back to facing forward, standing straight and tall.

Take a deep breath, in and out.

Take another slow breath, in and out.

Control Your Impulses

• • • • •

When you get angry, your body reacts as if it is in a dangerous situation. Perhaps someone said something mean to you or you got a bad grade on a test or your mom told you that you can't go to a party because you are grounded for something you did last week.

When you get angry, you may feel that your heart starts beating faster, your hands start sweating, your eyes fill up with tears, and you can feel the heat in your body rising. The phrase *my blood is boiling* reflects how when you are angry your blood moves faster in your body. You may feel like you want to hit something, say something out of anger, or run away from the situation. Often, though, when you react in this way, you have a greater chance of doing or saying something you'll regret.

An important part of being stronger in any situation is being able to control your impulses when you get angry or frustrated.

Here are some ideas for controlling your impulses in an angry moment:

• Take a deep breath, and use your breathing to control your body. You may want to put your hand on your heart, and breathe as you feel your heart beat.

• STOP: Stop, Take a deep breath, Observe your body, and Proceed. This exercise helps you slow down and get control.

• Separate yourself from the situation. Instead of just responding to a mean comment, walk away, so you can then decide the best way to respond once you can control your body.

• Count to ten before you respond.

The key to controlling your impulses in the long run is to be prepared beforehand with techniques that you can turn to when you need them. Practice the next exercise to get used to slowing down and collecting yourself before reacting to a situation.

FOUR BREATHS WITH MY FINGERS

- - - - - - - - - - - -

Time Needed: **1 MINUTE**
Location: **ANYTIME AND ANYWHERE**

In this exercise, you will breathe in and out while tapping your fingers.

You can practice this exercise throughout the day. When you need it in a moment of anger or frustration or panic, you will be ready to use the skills you've learned and practiced.

Begin with your left hand.

With your left thumb, touch the top of your left pinky and breathe in.

Now, use your same left thumb to touch the top of your left ring finger and breathe out.

Move the same left thumb to touch the top of your left middle finger and breathe in.

Finally, move the left thumb to touch the top of your left pointer finger and breathe out.

Now, let's use your right hand.

With your right thumb, touch the top of your right pinky and breathe in.

Now, use your same right thumb to touch the top of your right ring finger and breathe out.

Move your same right thumb to touch the top of your right middle finger and breathe in.

Finally, move your same right thumb to touch the top of your right pointer finger and breathe out.

Take Action

Stay Grounded

· · · · ·

The earth is a magical and magnificent place. You can see how grass, flowers, and trees grow from the earth; how water flows through it; and how it holds the sky and clouds.

The ground beneath your feet supports you. It is the ground on which you walk, on which our houses and schools and workplaces rest, and where most of us spend most of our time.

No matter how crazy life gets, how dizzy you may feel at times, or how you may seem to have too many feelings in one moment, you can use the ground beneath your feet to bring your body and emotions back to balance. You can put both feet on the ground and get anchored once again.

Actually taking off your shoes and socks and standing on the earth barefoot may give you energy, as well, and remind you that you're part of a world that is magnificent.

EXERCISE:

GET GROUNDED

- - - - - - - - - - - -

Time Needed: **5 TO 10 MINUTES**
Location: **INSIDE OR OUTSIDE**
Materials Needed: **A CHAIR ON WHICH, WHEN SITTING,
YOU CAN PUT YOUR FEET ON THE GROUND. IF YOU DON'T HAVE A CHAIR
THAT IS THE RIGHT SIZE, YOU CAN DO THIS EXERCISE STANDING.**

Sit comfortably in the chair.

Put your hands on your lap and put both feet flat on the ground.

Sit upright and, with your eyes open, let your eyes soften and look forward.

Take a deep breath in. Pause, and feel the ground beneath your feet. Breathe out. Say to yourself, "I feel grounded."

Still sitting in the chair, turn your neck to the left and gaze to the side. Take a deep breath in. Pause, and feel the ground beneath your feet. Breathe out and say to yourself, "I feel grounded."

Look back to center, and take a deep breath, in and out.

Sitting in the seat, turn your neck to the right and gaze to the side. Take a deep breath in. Pause, and feel the ground beneath your feet. Breathe out. Say to yourself, "I feel grounded."

Stand up tall.

Choose one direction to look in, perhaps forward.

With your hands hanging by your sides and your feet flat on the ground, look forward and take a deep breath in. Pause, and feel the ground beneath your feet. Breathe out. Say to yourself, "I feel grounded."

Turn your whole body to your left. Gaze forward. Take a deep breath in. Pause, and feel the ground beneath your feet. Breathe out. Say to yourself, "I feel grounded."

Turn your whole body left again (now you are facing backward). With your hands hanging by your sides and your feet flat on the ground, look forward. Take a deep breath in. Pause, and feel the ground beneath your feet. Breathe out. Say to yourself, "I feel grounded."

Take Action

Now, turn to your left again, to the final side (you should be back facing where you started). Gaze forward. Take a deep breath in. Pause, and feel the ground beneath your feet. Breathe out. Say to yourself, "I feel grounded."

Next time you are feeling like you need some stability, no matter where you are, standing or sitting, you can put your feet on the ground and say to yourself, "I feel grounded."

> If you are feeling closed up or tight inside, look upward. Imagine the sky above the roof and the stars above the sky. If you can, go outside and just look up!

Be Proactive

• • • • •

Being proactive means that you are self-motivated and do things before anyone else asks you to. When you take responsibility and do things on your own, you feel good about yourself, build confidence, and gain the respect of others. You become a stronger person and know better how to take your happiness and success into your own hands.

You can be proactive in your actions by taking care of where you live, by nurturing your body, and by reaching out to others. You can be proactive by making your bed, preparing your food or helping others prepare a meal, cleaning up after you eat or shower, taking out the trash, or helping do other chores.

You can also be proactive about your health by staying clean, drinking lots of water, eating well, moving a lot during the day, and making sure you get enough sleep.

You can be proactive in your community by reaching out to others, volunteering, or taking care of the environment.

> Mother Earth is your home. What can you do to take care of her?

WHAT CAN I TAKE RESPONSIBILITY FOR TODAY?

- - - - - - - - - -

Time Needed: **5 MINUTES**
Location: **SOMEWHERE YOU CAN THINK**
Materials Needed: **PAPER AND A PEN OR PENCIL**

Make a list of things you can do to be proactive to take care of yourself, others, or your environment. Break this list into three parts.

Easy: List the things that are easy for you to do by yourself. These may be things such as make my own bed, drink enough water, call my grandmother.

May Need Help: List the things you think you can do but that you may need some help with to accomplish. These may be things such as make my snack for school or load the dishwasher after dinner. Think of whom you can ask to support you.

One Day: Last, list the things you don't think you can do just yet, but that one day you aim to do! These may be things like babysit my younger brother or ride my bike to school. For now, don't worry about when you may do these—just set the intent (desire) that one day you will!

Get Organized

· · · · ·

You probably have a lot of things happening in your life—school, homework, taking care of family or siblings, sports, dance, martial arts, work, music, and hanging out with friends and family. Some people like to fill their days with activities and be around others, and some people prefer to be alone, reading a book, playing video games, shooting hoops, or playing with toys.

As life continues, you will have more and more things to do and more and more responsibilities. Knowing all that you have to do, and taking charge of your own schedule, is an important step to getting through what you have to do and making sure you have time to do the things you like to.

Take Action

CREATE A PLANNER

- - - - - - - - - -

Time Needed: **10 TO 15 MINUTES**
Location: **SOMEWHERE QUIET WHERE YOU CAN THINK**
Materials Needed: **PIECE OF PAPER AND A PEN**

For this exercise, let's just focus on the next week.

Write down the days of the week on the left side of the paper.

Under each day, put a line across the page. Give some space to write notes for each day.

Now go through each day and write what you have to do. For example, if you know you are in school from 8 a.m. to 3 p.m., write that down.

Then, write the activities and commitments you know you have each day. For example, if after school on Tuesdays you have a piano lesson, write 3:30 to 4:30 p.m.—Piano Lesson. Or if you play a sport, you can write Sports Practice for the days you know you need to be at school. For example, under Monday, Tuesday, and Thursday, you can write 3:30 to 5 p.m.—Basketball.

If you know you have special events, like a game or a recital or your grandmother's birthday party, write those in for the specific days.

Now, if you know that you need time to practice dance or flute, look at the days and times that are open and put this in.

If you need time for homework, you can think about what time you do that.

And, if your family has a set dinner time or daily or weekly commitment, list that, as well.

Remember that you need sleep to be happy and healthy. Write down what time you want or need to go to sleep to get at least nine hours of sleep each night.

Once you have filled in everything you know you have to do, look at your paper.

Think about if you are happy with your activities. You can also have a conversation with your parents or caretaker to make sure you all agree that your life has the right balance for you.

Just Feel

MONDAY Feed poncho

TUESDAY BRING A SNACK! · swim practice 3:30 - 4:30 pm

WEDNESDAY Feed poncho · ⭐ PICTURE DAY

THURSDAY swim practice 3:30 - 4:30 pm

FRIDAY ⭐ MATH TEST!!! · SCIENCE field trip permission slip due

SATURDAY Ava's B-day * PARTY * SLEEPOVER

SUNDAY Dinner at Aunt Kim's House 5:30 pm

Be Mindful of Your Spaces

● ● ● ●

Your spaces may be your backpack or closet, your desk at school or at home, where you sleep or eat or study, your room, or the bathroom you share with siblings.

It's really easy to let your spaces get messy and dirty.

Not all of us need a clean and orderly space to work and think in. Some of you may actually feel you think better in a chaotic space.

But being aware of your spaces and how they affect you can keep your mind clear and help you be more efficient. Making your bed, putting away your clothes, cleaning your bathroom, and keeping your homework in order may be things that dramatically help you stay more organized, waste less time, and keep you less frustrated by looking for things that are misplaced or hidden by other messes.

While you may not be able to control all your spaces, making sure the ones you can influence feel good for you can make you feel comforted and stable.

HOW CAN I SHAPE MY SPACES?

- - - - - - - - - - -

Time Needed: **5 MINUTES**
Materials Needed: **PAPER AND A PEN OR PENCIL**

Think of how you use space in your life.

It may be spaces where you keep things, like your closet, drawers, your backpack, or your desk at school.

It could be spaces where you physically spend time, like your bed, rooms in your house, classrooms, or outside.

There are some spaces that you can influence and others that you don't have much control over (maybe like a neighborhood park or a school assembly area).

List the spaces that you **can** *influence.*

Next to each space, write down how you would like it to feel.

Think about colors, objects, cleanliness, and what you can do to make that space right for you.

If you share a space with others, reach out to them and think about how together you can make that space feel special. Figuring out how you want a space to feel with someone else is a good way to learn how to express your point of view and to come to an agreement about what would work best for you both. Once you have agreed on some sort of plan, decide specifically what each one of you will do to make that space special!

Can you feel what's going on in a room? Try just observing what's going on around you and see if you can sense other people's feelings.

Take Action

Do Something Nice for Someone Else

• • • • •

We all feel lonely at times. We all feel sad. We all feel frustrated.

And while it is completely normal to have these feelings, sometimes you can get stuck just feeling bad or sad about your life.

One way to try to change your bad mood is to do something for someone else—something that you don't have to do, that you don't even expect a thank-you or payback for, but something that just makes someone else happier.

Perhaps you can go visit an elderly person in your neighborhood and sit with them for twenty minutes.

Or you can bake something special for your family.

Or you can decide that you are going to give compliments to five different people.

Or you may decide you are going to write a letter to your grandfather or someone else in your family.

Perhaps you ask your younger sibling to play a game with you.

Or you decide to clean the dishes before your parents get home from work so that they can relax.

Or you go outside and pick up trash from the sidewalk.

Or you say a prayer for the health and happiness of your classmates.

When you do something nice for someone else with no expectation for anything in return, you can feel good about yourself. When you see how your actions can make someone else smile, you feel the power you have to make others feel better. And, in turn, you will feel better, too!

Take Action

HOW CAN I HELP SOMEONE ELSE TODAY?

- - - - - - - - - - - -

Time Needed: **DEPENDS ON WHAT YOU WANT TO DO**

Think of something you can do today to make someone else happier.

Decide how and when you are going to do it, but commit to doing it right now or before the end of the day.

Commit to yourself that you are doing this just because you want to. You don't need a thank-you, and perhaps you don't even need to tell anyone what you did.

Then, go out and do the thing you set out to do.

At the end of the day, before you go to sleep, put your attention on your heart and think about how helping someone else made you feel.

Express Yourself to Yourself

• • • • •

Sometimes you just need to cry or scream or laugh hysterically to let out your feelings.

But other times you may hold back your feelings, because it is hard to open up what may be a floodgate of emotion. It is also normal to block big feelings, as you may be scared to let them out or to admit to having them to others or to yourself. Sometimes someone else's words or actions may make you want to shut down your feelings.

Being with your feelings, even when it is hard, is a healthy way to process them. But it is important for your health that you do what feels safest for you. If your feelings feel too big, it may be a good idea to turn to a parent, therapist, or school counselor for help.

Some people find that writing, singing, drawing, dancing, or doing creative projects help them to more gently process their feelings.

EXERCISE:

DRAW MY FEELINGS

- - - - - - - - - -

Time Needed: **HOWEVER LONG YOU WANT**
Materials Needed: **PAPER, CRAYONS, COLORED PENCILS, PAINT,
OR WHATEVER YOU MAY HAVE OR WANT TO USE**

Get your materials in order and find a quiet, safe place where you can enjoy this project.

Before you begin, take a deep breath and just be in the present moment.

You may find that a feeling comes up from earlier in the day—something that made you happy or sad, frustrated, angry, or super excited.

Breathe in and out again.

Now, without feeling as if you need to draw anything specific, pick up your materials and start drawing. Grab the colors that you feel connected to in this moment.

Scribble. Draw shapes or lines of structures. Change colors as you need to. Note how different colors may make you feel.

Just be as free as possible as you draw.

You do not need to share this drawing with anyone. Just use the time to give yourself space and to feel.

Drawing, painting, making collages, or other forms of art can help you relax, let go, and express yourself in different ways. Sometimes you may find that you draw something and realize that it is an expression of a feeling you were having that you were not even aware of. If you choose to share your drawings with someone you trust, it may be a nice way to talk about what you feel when you look at it again.

Take Action

Write It Out!

• • • • •

For some people, writing out your feelings is a great way to process and release them.

You may find that you like to write creative stories or a song. Or you may like to write about what happened during your day, describing events and feelings in detail. You may like to write poems or just a list of words.

Finding time to write in a personal journal can become a special time for you to process your feelings. When you write in your journal, you should absolutely feel like you can write whatever you want without judgement. If it's important that your words are private, make sure you tell your parents, siblings, or others where you live that they cannot look in your journal. You can ask them to respect your privacy.

Find poems, lyrics to songs, and quotes that make you happy.

EXERCISE:

CREATE A JOURNAL

- - - - - - - - - - -

Time Needed: AS LONG AS YOU WANT FOR
HOWEVER LONG AS YOU WANT
Materials Needed: A NOTEBOOK OR PIECES OF PAPER, AND A PEN,
PENCIL, MARKERS, OR COLORED PENCILS

Find a notebook or blank book that you can write in. Perhaps you have an old school notepad that has blank pieces of paper in it. You could ask for a journal as a gift. Another option is to write on sheets of loose leaf paper and collect them in a folder or keep them in a special place in your room.

Decorate your journal to make it personal and just for you. You may use stickers or draw on it; or maybe you prefer to keep it clean and plain. Whatever you do, treat it as something special.

When you sit down to write in your journal, remember that this is your space. This is not an assignment, and no one will grade you on what you write. You can write whatever you want. You can experiment. You can be truthful or you can simply make up stories and let your imagination go wild. Write whatever you want that helps you release your feelings. You may find you want to laugh or cry. Whatever you are feeling is okay and right for you at this moment.

Finding a regular time to write in your journal can be a nice and reassuring practice. Sometimes it is also helpful and fun (and funny!) to go back and read what you wrote a month or even a year ago!

Take Action

Be Part of Something Bigger

· · · · ·

Sometimes when you feel really lonely, it is helpful to remember you are part of something more than just yourself. There are, in fact, generations of people who came before you.

In American Indian traditions, when a person makes an important decision, they ask themselves, "What would those who came before me do?" They also think about how their actions will affect their children, their children's children, and their children's children's children.

When you think of yourself as part of a continuum of several generations, you can reflect on how the people before you struggled and laughed and loved and had feelings just like you. And those that come after you, they, too, will have stories that you shape.

HOW CAN I HELP MY WORLD?

- - - - - - - - - - - - -

Time Needed: **10 MINUTES**
Materials Needed: **PAPER AND PEN**

On a sheet of paper, write the word ME in the middle.

Around the word ME, begin to list the groups that you are part of. You can write things like:

- *My Family*
- *My School*
- *My Friends*
- *My Sports Team*
- *My Girl Scout/Boy Scout Troop*
- *My Apartment Building*

- *My Church/My Temple/My Synagogue/My Mosque*
- *My Neighborhood*
- *My City*
- *My Country*
- *My Planet*
- *My Solar System*

After you have listed your groups, reflect on how you can contribute to, support, and help others in your groups.

For example, think about something you can do for your family that may be appreciated—like doing extra chores or teaching your grandfather how to use his phone or reading to your little sister before she goes to bed.

For your school, neighborhood, or city, perhaps you can think about ways you can make it feel cleaner or safer. Can you volunteer to help in a local nursing home or help a neighbor shovel the snow from their driveway or walk their dog?

Think about how you can help your community and planet. Could you create posters to encourage people to recycle?

Write down your ideas next to the appropriate category.

Commit to doing at least one thing on your list in a certain timeframe (perhaps in the next week or month).

Just Feel

AFTERWORD BY DEEPAK CHOPRA

Our experience of the world starts with *being* and unfolds as *feeling*, *thinking*, and *doing*. Unfortunately, as we look around us, we see that most of the adults in our lives (perhaps even our parents) have become *human doings* instead of *human beings*.

Every living creature, not just humans, navigates experience through feeling, which is the most fundamental way to know and sense the world. When we lose the ability to genuinely connect with others at a basic level through the most nourishing emotions of love, compassion, empathy, and joy, we literally lose touch with our innermost being.

Our emotions are the most important cause of our physical well-being. Our feelings are both mental and bodily experiences. If you are joyful and happy, your body will be strong and energetic, and you will also notice that your mind is more alert, curious, and full of wonder and creativity. In other words, your feelings are important in helping decide the quality of your life as you grow up.

If you look at life all around you, every living being is seeking feelings of joy or happiness. True success comes to those who have the ability to love and have compassion, and this is also the secret to fulfilling your goals as you grow up.

In this book, you learned the basics of how to have healthy feelings by listening to the messages in your body, because your emotions are sensations coupled with thoughts. As you think about the simple techniques that Mallika has shown you in these different chapters, you can rest assured that cultivating emotional and social intelligence is the best way for you to prepare for the adventure and challenges that life will offer to you as you begin your journey through your childhood, teenage years, and into adulthood.

The great mathematician-philosopher Blaise Pasquel said, "We know the truth not only by the reason but also by the heart." Throughout the ages, poets, philosophers, sages, and great teachers have said that our most intimate, true, and authentic feelings can heal the wounds caused by stressful and excessive thinking.

My hope is that as the future leaders of the world, you will learn to be intimate with your feelings, to bond emotionally with those whom you share a higher vision, and to create a world that is healthier, joyful, holy, and healed.

Deepak Chopra

RESOURCES

The following books inspired me as a parent and author to explore social and emotional intelligence, grit, resilience, well-being, and joy.

Grit: The Power of Passion and Perseverance, by Angela Duckworth

Quiet: The Power of Introverts in a World That Can't Stop Talking, by Susan Cain

Resilient: How to Grow an Unshakable Core of Calm, Strength, and Happiness, by Rick Hanson

HBR Guide to Emotional Intelligence, by Harvard Business Review Press

How to Win Friends and Influence People, by Dale Carnegie

Nonviolent Communication: A Language of Life, by Marshall B. Rosenberg

The Gift of Failure: How the Best Parents Learn to Let Go So Their Children Can Succeed, by Jessica Lahey

It's Not Always Depression : A New Theory of Listening to Your Body, Discovering Core Emotions and Reconnecting with Your Authentic Self, by Hilary Jacobs Hendel, LCSW

Wellbeing: The Five Essential Elements, by Tom Rath and Jim Harter

Your Happiest You: The Care & Keeping of Your Mind and Spirit, by Judy Woodburn and published by American Girl

ACKNOWLEDGMENTS

I'd like to thank the kids and teachers who have welcomed me into their classrooms to explore how we can breathe, be more mindful, express gratitude, and set intentions. You have taught me so much from your comments and questions and have shown me that learning with laughter and silliness can be most powerful!

For this book, I shared the manuscript with a small group of people whom I trust when it comes to emotional intelligence for children. Thank you to Kanika Priya Sethi, MeLissa Gavarette, and Kaarina Roberto for reading the draft manuscript with a quick turnaround time and for giving me invaluable notes and exercises. My deepest gratitude to my dad, Deepak Chopra, who is the first person in our family to read or listen or watch anything my brother and I do. Needless to say, this book is inspired by his work and the many lessons he and my mom, Rita Chopra, have taught our family.

Thank you again to MeLissa, who continues to make sure I do what I need to do, and to Geeta Singh who patiently explores and manages all the details for my speaking opportunities. I'm so excited to be working with Aaron Marion on PR—he has hit it out of the ballpark! Thank you to my amazing literary agent, Linda Loewenthal, who has been looking out for me for fifteen years now! And to the team at Running Press—Kristin Kiser, Julie Matysik, Valerie Howlett, Frances Soo Ping Chow—once again, you have been absolutely fabulous to work with!

And it goes without saying that Brenna Vaughan creates the magic here, as she did for *Just Breathe*—she has brought life to the material with her illustrations in a way that is comforting and joyful!

Of course, I am forever grateful to my daughters, Tara and Leela, and my husband, Sumant Mandal. This time as I was writing the book, the girls had loads of homework and tests (ahh, high school!), black-belt testing, and lots of life planning, and Sumant kept it all together for us, making breakfast every day as always and working at the same time!

Also Available from Mallika Chopra
and Running Press Kids:

Available wherever books and ebooks are sold!